GOD DESCENDS ON EARTH

GOD DESCENDS ON EARTH

SANJAY KANT

PUBLISHING

© Sri Sathya Sathya Sai Towers Hotels (P) Ltd

All rights reserved. No part of this publication may be reproduced or transmitted in any form or by any means, electronic or mechanical, including photocopy, without permission in writing from the publisher. Reviewers may quote brief passages.

Reprint 1998

ISBN-81-86822-58-5

Published & Distributed by:
Sai Towers Publishing
(A Unit of Sri Sathya Sai Towers Hotels Pvt Ltd.)
3/497 Main Road
Prasanthi Nilayam - 515 134
INDIA
Tel : 91-8555-87880
Fax : 91-8555-87302
EMail : saitower@giasbg01.vsnl.net.in

Contact for Mail Order in U.S.A.
JAI SAI RAM
PO Box 900
Trinidad, CO 81082 U.S.A.
Phone : (719) 846-0846
Fax : (719) 846-0847
E-Mail : jaisairm @ ria.net
OR
jaisairm @ rmi.net

Distributors in Australia:
Mr James Somers
13 Hunter street, Parramatta, NSW 2150
Ph : 0061 2 9687 2441
Fax : 0061 2 9687 2449

Distributors in West Indies:
Ace Printery Fed Traders Ltd.,
34-36, Pasea Main Road
Tunapuna, Trinidad & Tobago
Tel/Fax : (868) 663-CARD (2273), 663-2152, 3223
E-mail : ramdhan@trinidad.net

Printed by:
D.K. Fine Arts Press Pvt. Ltd.
New Delhi - 110 052

This book is dedicated to the memory of the author, Sanjay Kant who attained Baba's Lotus Feet on 6th June 1995

CONTENTS

1. The Prophets 1

2. Advent of the Lord 7

3. Almighty Power 25

4. Three Temporal Kings 35

5. The Great Law Giver 39

6. Ornate Speeches 47

7. The Last Word 65

Glossary 70

THE PROPHETS

NOSTRADAMUS

16th Century French Prophet Nostradamus was a doctor by profession. He graduated in medicine from the University of Montpellier in France. His unorthodox ways of curing plague victims brought him a lot of fame. His interests also grew in Astrology and the occult and he developed remarkable psychic ability. His fame as a psychic and an astrologer grew far and wide.

Once travelling through Italy, Nostradamus passed a young monk. He knelt down in front of this monk and called him "Your Holiness". All those around were surprised by this gesture. This monk later became Pope Sixtus V.

During the later part of his life Nostradamus decided to write prophecies concerning the future of the world. He published this work in 1555. He wrote that he purposely confused the time sequence of these prophecies so that they could not be easily decoded. He did this to avoid prosecution by the Church. This publication made Nostradamus even more famous throughout Europe.

Queen Catherine de Medici invited Nostradamus to discuss a prophecy he had made concerning Henri II. Nostradamus had predicted that Henri II would die in a duel. The reply pleased the Queen for she became a believer in Nostradamus till her death. Henri II did die in a game of duel. His death was very tragic just as had been prophesied by Nostradamus.

Nostradamus was so famous that foreign ambassadors in France wrote to their kings and queens about his prophecies. His fame and legend lives to this day.

Hitler's attention was drawn to the fact that he was mentioned in some of Nostradamus prophecies. In 1940, the German Air Force started air dropping forged and altered quatrains from various Nostradamus prophecies, The aim was to demoralise the enemy forces and their civilians. These forged prophecies predicted Hitler's victory in the War. To counter this the British Intelligence also faked Nostradamus prophecies and launched a massive counter propaganda by air dropping these over France and other countries. The British Intelligence is believed to have spent an enormous amount of money for this counter propaganda.

A Nostradamus prophecy, which has recently come to pass, predicted the present Gulf crisis. Nostradamus prophesied that when U.S.A. and Russia become friends there will be turmoil and bloodshed in the Middle East. He also foresaw the destruction of Hiroshima by Atom bomb. He predicted Hitler and Napoleon's rise to power, the Iranian revolution by the Ayatollah, the rise and fall of the British Empire, the turmoils in France and other countries during the world wars and the Russian Revolution. These are only few of his prophecies which have come to pass.

EDGAR CAYCE

Edgar Cayce (1877-1945) has been hailed as America's greatest psychic prophet. He would lie down on a couch and then go into a self induced state of trance. Psychic Cayce would then sleep talk. He would answer questions on a variety of subject matters. A secretary was always available to take notes in shorthand. This phenomenon of sleep talking is called a 'reading'. Cayce would not remember anything he said during the trance. He had to be told about the contents of the reading after he woke up from trance. During the course of a reading Cayce could diagnose a person's medical problem and also suggest a remedy. Even some doctors recommended their patients to him. Cayce remedies are now popular with doctors and patients alike. During trance Cayce would also answer questions on reincarnation, past lives, E.S.P., spirituality, evolution of life on earth, diet and nutrition, inter-personal relationships and also future events.

Cayce predicted the world economic crisis of 1929. He foresaw events leading to and following the Second World War. He saw the coming independence of India. Cayce also had the power of Retrocognition-the ability to see past events. He described how pyramids were built. His account of various past civilizations and the submerging of Atlantis is startling.

Edgar Cayce foresaw a free religious Russia. In a reading he said that the great hope of the world will emerge from Russia. Even his ardent admirers would not have expected that this prophecy would come true. Recent developments in Russia and Eastern Europe have however shocked the world. The situation in these countries is still in a state of flux. Cayce also predicted that U.S. and Russia will become friends. Nobody, even in his wildest dream, expected this to happen.

Cayce's psychic phenomenon was not only unique but remarkable. During trance he would somehow bypass his conscious mind and tune in to the super-conscious mind. This means that Cayce's conscious mind did not interpret the information coming from the super-conscious mind. This certainly makes misinterpretation impossible. Most other psychics have to rely on their conscious mind to interpret the visions they see and hear. Sometimes their personal opinions and prejudices may hamper or even alter the interpretation of their visions. The conscious mind has its own limitations. If you close your eyes and try to visualize infinite space in the Universe, the chances are that the conscious mind may spring a boundary around this infinite space. Such are the limitations of the conscious mind. This factor may also impede correct interpretation of a psychic vision. Cayce's psychic phenomenon was, therefore, certainly unique. This also explains why some of Cayce readings were contrary to his personal beliefs.

Both Nostradamus and Edgar Cayce were God fearing men. They acknowledged that their psychic phenomenon was the gift of God. These two men genuinely wanted to help people rather than display their psychic talent for money. Nostradamus served people as a doctor and Cayce helped cure people through his psychic gift. They would always be remembered as the greatest psychics of all times.

SAINT AUROBINDO

Shri Aurobindo needs no introduction in India. He was one of the most enlightened saints of the 20th Century. Psychic powers came naturally to him because of his spiritual enlightenment. He saw visions during the state of spiritual trance.

He foresaw India's independence and partition. He also

predicted the subsequent partition of Pakistan (India liberated Bangladesh from Pakistan during 1971 military operations). He also foresaw change in India's leadership in 1984. Again, he was right because in 1984 Rajiv Gandhi became Prime Minister after Indira Gandhi's assassination. Indira Gandhi was virtually India's Prime Minister for almost two decades.

LACHHMAN DAS MADAN

Madan is not a psychic. He bases his predictions on the ancient Indian system of astrology. He is a retired Government official who now devotes a lot of time predicting world events.

Months before the events actually took place, Madan predicted that the United States would get involved in serious military operations within 6 weeks from 20th June, 1990. When Madan made this prediction the cold war was over and Eastern Europeans were basking in the light of their new found freedom. There was no tension in the world to warrant serious military operations by the U.S. Forces. On 2nd August, 1990, Iraq surprised the world by invading Kuwait. Massive U.S. Forces have since been deployed in the Gulf region. This is America's largest force deployment since the Vietnam war.

Madan successfully predicted U.S. air attack on Libya, the assassination of Indira Gandhi, death of Pakistan President Zia-ul-Haque, overthrow of Benazir Bhutto regime in Pakistan, India's military intervention in Sri Lanka, death of Khomeni and the change of Indian Government in 1989. He also predicted that V.P. Singh would become Prime Minister of India. These are only few of his successful predictions.

Madan has been hailed by the Indian press for his remarkably accurate predictions.

ADVENT OF THE LORD

The Hindus are looking forward to the advent of an Avatar -the descent of God in human form, the Christians await the second coming and the Buddhists anticipate the coming of Maitreya. There have also been many prophecies predicting the emergence of a Divine Messiah towards the close of this century. Nostradamus made many prophecies describing the birth place of this Divine Entity, his mission and attributes. Nostradamus also gave us clues so that we can identify this Divine personality, whom he considers the Second Coming of Christ. Sri Aurobindo announced the date of birth of an Avatar. He learned about this Advent in a state of spiritual trance and Edgar Cayce gave us the time period during which the world should expect the emergence of a Universal Messiah.

Astrologer Lachhman Das Madan has made some similar predictions in his book *Astrological Predictions of the Major Countries of the World-The next twenty years* 1990-2010(1990 Edition). In prediction No.51 of this book he writes "A very important religious leader will emerge on the scene who will receive universal respect and spread the message of peace, prosperity and one world." This prediction is for India for the period March, 1991 to April, 1992. In prediction, No.246 for India, covering the period April 1998 to April 1999, he writes: "A religious saint may demonstrate real spiritual enlightenment and may receive the attention and respect of the whole world."

In a prophecy Edgar Cayce said that there will be great changes between 1958 and 1998, "when these will be proclaimed as period when His light will be seen again in the clouds." Cayce also foresaw the emergence of a Universal Messiah around the period 1998. "When those that have gradually forgotten God entirely have been eliminated, and there has come, and there will come at the close of this next year, the period when there will be no part of the Globe where man has not had the opportunity to hear, 'THE LORD, HE IS GOD,' and when this period has been accomplished, the new era, the new age, is to begin." Cayce readings say that this would come to pass around 1998 A.D.

The obvious question is: Where is this Messiah? Cayce refers to him as God and Madan ascribes him with true spiritual enlightenment. Both Cayce and Madan also agree that this Messiah will have world-wide influence and that he will be universally accepted. If this messiah is to emerge on the world scene during the next few years it would mean that he has already taken birth. Sri Aurobindo confirms this theory. In the book *Sri Aurobindo on Himself and the Mother*, he writes: "24th November, 1926, was the descent of Krishna into the physical." "A power infallible shall lead the thought. In earthly hearts kindle the Immortal's Fire, even the multitude shall hear the Voice". We have Sri Aurobindo declaring that this Messiah is no other than Lord Krishna-the Supreme personality of Godhead.

At this stage, let us consider three Nostradamus prophecies. They describe the Second Coming theme.

He, who has been awaited for such a long time, will never appear in Europe. He will appear in Asia. One from the league issued from the great Hermes. His power will rise over all other Kings in the Eastern Countries.

X. 75.

NOSTRADAMUS

Nostradamus reference to Hermes, the Greek messenger of the gods, is a clear clue that this prophecy relates to the advent of a Divine Principle. According to this prophecy this Divine Entity will appear in Asia and not in Europe. He further elaborates that this Divine Power will rise over all other kings in the Eastern countries. The first line of this quatrain suggests the 'Second Coming.' Nostradamus, 16th century Catholic background is also evident as he tries to interpret the vision he saw.

Let us consider another Nostradamus prophecy.

The triplicity of waters will give birth to a Man who will choose Thursday as his Holy day. His voice, reign and power will rise across land and sea, amid storms in the East.

1.50

NOSTRADAMUS

The last line of this quatrain undoubtedly is linked with the last line of the previous quatrain X.75. Nostradamus, in this prophecy, elaborates that the Divine personality who will appear in Asia, will be born in a peninsula or a place surrounded by three different waters or seas. This Divine Man will choose Thursday as his holy day. Nostradamus again asserts that the Power of this personality will rise across land and sea. This will happen when there are turmoils in the Eastern countries.

Surprisingly no religion observes Thursday as its day of worship. Muslims offer prayers on Friday, Jews on Saturday, Christians on Sunday and although Hindus have no specific day for worship, some Hindu deities are specially worshipped on Monday, Tuesday, Friday and Saturday. Wednesdays and Thursdays are the odd ones out.

The next Nostradamus prophecy is equally interesting.

The earth and air will freeze so much water, when all will come to worship on Thursdays. What will be was never so beautiful before. From all parts of the world they will come to honour HIM.

X.71

NOSTRADAMUS

Here Nostradamus continues from the previous mentioned quatrain 1.50. He predicts that the Divine Man, who will choose Thursday as his holy day, will be worshipped by all on Thursdays. This suggests world-wide influence of this Divine person. Nostradamus adds that people from all parts of the world will come to honour this Divine Man. The whole quatrain suggests the Advent of a Universal Messiah. The first line of this quatrain may have been used metaphorically to describe the importance or sanctity of future worship, by all, on Thursdays.

These three prophecies are undoubtedly interlinked. To sum it up, a Universal Messiah will appear in Asia. He will choose Thursday as his holy day. He will be born in a place surrounded by three seas. All people from all parts of the world will come to honour him. These are the major clues that Nostradamus offers besides adding that his name, rule and power will grow across land and sea.

Nostradamus made these prophecies in the 16th century. Almost 400 years later, on 23rd May, 1940, a thirteen year old boy named Sathya Narayana Raju (of Puttaparthi village in India) called his family around him. With a mere wave of his hand he materialized, as if from nowhere, some sugarcandy and flowers for them. Hearing this, the neighbours rushed in to see the miracle. Sathya materialized sugarcandy and flowers for them too. He then surprised everyone by announcing- "I am Sai Baba... I have come to ward off all your troubles; keep your houses clean and pure." His father was not at all impressed by all this. In dismay he asked Sathya "What are we to do with you?" Sathya replied "Worship me." "The dumbfounded father asked, "When?" Pat came the answer, "Every THURSDAY."

On 20th October, 1940, 13 year old Sathya Narayana or Sai Baba, as he called himself, came back early from school. He set his books aside and then told his family, "I don't belong to you, my work is waiting; my devotees are calling me. I can't stay any longer; I do not consider myself related to you." These words came from a teenage boy who was to turn fourteen a month later. Sathya Narayana then left the house and moved into the garden of the Excise Inspector's house. Villagers, who had seen his 'miracles', converged to him.

Nobody in the village had heard the name 'Sai Baba' before. Later, it was found that Sai Baba was a mystic saint who lived in Shirdi (at present in the State of Maharashtra, India). This mystic saint was famous for his miraculous power. Sai Baba of Shirdi left his body in 1918 saying that he would reincarnate after eight years. He was regarded by his devotees as an Avatar- the descent of God in human form.

Thirteen year old Sathya Narayana claimed that he was the reincarnation of Sai Baba of Shirdi. At the request of his devotees Sathya Narayana assumed the name Sathya Sai Baba so as to distinguish himself from Sai Baba of Shirdi.

Today Sathya Sai Baba is worshipped by over 50 million people from all parts of the world. This is an unofficial estimate and the actual figures may be many times more. Sai Baba devotees are not part of any cult or organisation and therefore, it is difficult to estimate their number. Many of these have never seen him, which makes any head count an impossible task.

Millions of Hindus consider him to be an Avatar-descent of the Lord in human form. He is worshipped by Hindus, Christians, Jews, Muslims and Buddhists alike. His devotees include Presidents and Prime Ministers of few countries, Federal and State Ministers, Governors, Ambassadors, Military Generals, U.N. delegates, Hollywood personalities, top doctors, scientists, eminent judges and of course millions of ordinary people from U.S.A., Canada, South America, Europe, Africa, Asia and Australia. Thursday is the day of special prayers and fasting for Sai Baba devotees.

Is Sathya Sai Baba the Messiah promised by the Prophets? He was born on 23rd November, 1926. Sri Aurobindo declared that the Krishna Incarnate was born on 24th November, 1926. After 64 years of this announced date, it does seem that Sri Aurobindo did actually refer to Sathya Sai Baba's advent. Nostradamus mentioned that tha Lord will appear in Asia. Sathya Sai Baba was born in the Indian sub-continent of Asia. Nostradamus also described the Lord's birth place as being surrounded by three seas. Sai Baba was born in Puttaparthi (District Anantapur, State of Andhra Pradesh). Puttaparthi is part of the Indian Peninsula, surrounded by the waters of Bay of Bengal in East, Arabian Sea in West and Indian Ocean in South. As prophesied by Nostradamus, Sathya Sai Baba chose Thursday as his holy day. Let us not forget that he was only thirteen when he declared Thursday as his holy day. It is also true that people from all parts of the world come to honour him.

According to an article published in *Two Worlds* magazine of London, an Iranian writer was irresistibly drawn to a huge volume in Tehran. This Book, called *The Ocean of Light*, is in 25 volumes. It is claimed to be the collection of the discourses of Prophet Mohammed. Volume 13 of these discourses is called "Mehedi Moud" in Arabic, meaning "The Great teacher that was promised." The teacher is also referred to as "Master of the World", "Master of Time", "God's President" and "God Speaking and Advising". Prophet Mohammed is quoted by Peggy Mason to have indicated a large number of signs or marks by which the great teacher would be recognised. Prominent among these hallmarks, which remarkably identify with Sathya Sai Baba are: "His hair will be profuse. His forehead will be large and conclave. His nose will be small, with a slight bump at the bridge. His front teeth will be spaced apart. He will have a mole on his cheek, He will not have a beard but will be clean shaven. His clothing will be like a flame. He will wear two robes (one an under robe). The colour of his face will be some times yellow like gold, some times very dark and some times shining like the moon. His body will be small. His legs will be like those of a young girl. All the teachings of all the religions of the world will be in his heart from birth. All the science and knowledge of the world from the beginning of the time will be in his heart.

"All things which you will ask from God, He (the Master of the World) will give you. All the treasures are under his feet. He will give gifts that are light in weight. He will go around among his devotees and touch their heads with his hand. Every eye that sees him will be happy, not only humans but disembodied souls. He will live 95 years" (Sai Baba has said that he will be in the present body for 95 years-this means he would leave his present body around 2020 A.D.).

"In the last 20 years of his life he will be the "King of the whole world", but at that time only two-thirds of the people of the world will believe in him (This period would then be 2000 A.D.- corraborating Cayce Prophecies). Muslims will recognise him only nine years before his passing from the world. He will make the world light and full of peace. So as not to be deceived, you should know that the Master of the World will bring things out of His body, through His Mouth."

Sai Baba does bring out Shivalings on Shivratri every year. The Shivalings come out of his mouth. Although now he does not bring out Shivalings in public, earlier hundreds of thousands used to gather to see the spectacle. This manifestation of Shivalings can be seen in many Sai Baba video films recorded earlier.

An obvious question is: What does Sathya Sai Baba say about himself? Does he claim that he is God? The author has compiled certain relevant extracts from Sai Baba's discourses. The following extracts may answer some of our questions:

"The totality of Divine Energy has come unto humanity as Sathya Sai......." "....... This is a human form in which every Divine Entity, every Divine Principle, that is to say, all the names and forms ascribed by man to God are manifest."

"Whenever there is a languishing of Dharma or righteousness and an upheaval of unrighteousness, I create Myself, for it is part of Primal resolution or Sankalpa to protect the spiritual structure of the universe. I lay aside My formless essence and assume a name and a form suited to the purpose for which I come. Whenever evil threatens to vanquish good, I have to come and save it from decline."

"In order that you may attain the only goal of human life, namely, realising the Divine and becoming Divine, the Eternal has limited itself and come in this human Form. It will reveal the ideals again, and re-establish it among all men. Of course, it is difficult for those who are unacquainted with the scriptures to grasp the mystery of this advent."

"The meaning of Avatar is this: to save mankind. God out of His Love, affection and compassion, comes down to the level of man and arouses the Divine Consciousness in man. He makes man aware of Him when He finds him desperately searching outside of himself for Him who is his very core."

"The Avatar behaves in a human way so that mankind can feel kinship but, rises to super-human heights so that mankind can aspire to those heights."

"In each Yuga, the Divine has incorporated itself as an Avatar for some particular task. This incarnation is different in that it has to deal with the crisis which is world-wide and world-shaking. Intellectual conceit has grown so wild that men have become foolish enough to ask, 'What and where is God?' Immorality has put on the garb of morality and is enticing man into the morass of sin. Truth is condemned as a trap; justice is jeered at; saints are harassed as social enemies. Hence this incarnation has come to uphold the True and suppress the False. I behave like you, moving, singing, laughing, journeying, but watch out for the blow I inflict all of a sudden, to chastise and to warn. I shall scorch the wrong-doer for his wrong and soothe the virtuous for his righteousness."

"Since I move about with you, eat like you, and talk with you, you are deluded into the belief that this is but an instance of common humanity. Be warned against this mistake. I am also deluding you by My singing with you, talking with you, and engaging Myself in activities with you. But, any moment, My Divinity may be revealed to you; you have to be ready, prepared for that moment. Since Divinity is enveloped by human-ness you must endeavour to overcome the Maya (Delusion) that hides it from your eyes."

"I eat as you do, move about as you do, talk in your language and behave as you can understand, for your sake, not for My sake. I direct you towards the Divine, winning your confidence, your love, your loyalty, by being among you, as one of you. My aim is to transmute you into spiritual aspirants so as to enable you to know your true being, becoming aware of the Truth of the Universe, which is but a projection of your own Truth".

"I do not claim that I am a Guru or, consider you as Disciples or pupils. When I am All that is, who can be separately specified as Guru and who as Disciple or pupil? Ignorance of the One leads one to this dischotomy. Realisation of the Truth will end this distinction. None need teach, none need learn. All are fundamentally Chith. This is the Reality."

"Your worldly intelligence cannot fathom the ways of God. He cannot be recognised by mere cleverness, which is what your intelligence mostly is. You may benefit from God, but you cannot explain Him."

"Your explanations are merely guesses, attempts to clothe your ignorance in pompous expressions. The mistake is, you give the brain more value than it deserves."

"Do not spend your time trying to understand Me; do not waste your time in the attempt. The reason why I am saying this is: It is beyond any one's capacity to understand Me. So, trying to do the impossible, you are only wasting your time and your effort. It is only when you succeed in knowing yourselves that you can know Me. I need nothing, however great or small, in this Universe. At no moment has desire affected me for anything or activity. I am the person come to give, not to receive. And, what you can offer me is just this: pure, unadulterated Love. When you offer me that, I derive Ananda."

"In truth, you cannot understand the nature of My Reality either today, or even after a thousand years of steady austerity or ardent inquiry even if all mankind joins in that effort. But, in a short time, you will become cognisant of the Bliss showered by the Divine Principle, which has taken upon itself this sacred body, and this sacred Name. Your good fortune which will provide you this chance is greater than what was available for anchorites, monks, sages, saints and even personalities embodying facets of Divine Glory!"

"This is a pot; this a thatch; this a house; this a wall; this a jungle; this a hill; this the ground; this the lake; this the fire; this the wind; this the sky; this the maker of the day; this the light; these the stars; these the planets; these the inert, these the vital; this is he, that is his person; these are all distinct from me; this material world is different from me-thus as a witness, I cognise all this and fill each with the principle of existence without the help of any disciplinary process, for I am above and beyond all this."

"Rama and Krishna and Sai Baba appear different because of the dress each has donned, but it is the Self-same Entity believe Me. Do not be misled into error and loss."

"I know your past, I know your future. So I know why you suffer and how you can escape suffering and when you finally will. I know everything that has happened to everybody in the past, everything that is happening and everything that will happen in the future. I know why a person has to suffer in this life and what will happen to him the next time he is born because of that suffering this time." For Me, there is no native land or foreign land. All humanity has to be brought back to the path of Dharma."

"I shall not not give you up, even if you forsake Me; for it is not in Me to forsake those who deny me. I have come for all. Those who stray away will come again to me, do not doubt this. I shall beckon them back to me.

"Come just one step forward, I shall take a hunderd toward you. Shed just one tear, I shall wipe a hundred from your eyes."

"I am you! You are me! That is the Truth and you will realise it when you reach the goal. You are the waves and I am the Ocean."

"Revere any Name; the reverence reaches me, for, I answer to all Names. Denigrate any individual; it affects me; for all individuals are expressions of My Will."

"I answer to whatever Name you use; I respond to whatever request you make with a pure heart and a sanctified motive."

"Along the lines already familiar to you, continue the worship of the God of your choice; then you will find that you are coming nearer and nearer to Me; for, all Names are Mine and all Forms are Mine. There is no need to change, after you have seen Me and heard Me."

"You call Me by One Name only and believe I have One Form only. Remember, there is no Name I do not bear, there is no Form which is not Mine."

"I do not encourage this adoration of just one Name and one Form, and that too, My present Name and My present Form. I have no wish to draw people towards Me, away from the worship of My other Names and Forms. You may infer from what you call My miracles, that I am causing them to attract and to attach you to Me, and Me alone. They are not intended do demonstrate or publicise; they are merely spontaneous and concomitant proofs of Divine Majesty. I am yours; you are mine, for ever and ever. What need is there for attracting and impressing, for demonstrating your Love or My compassion? I am in you; you are in Me. There is no distance or distinction."

"I never call upon people to worship Me, giving up the Forms they already revere. I have come to establish Dharma and so I do not and will not demand or require your homage. Give it to your Lord or Guru, whoever He is; I am the Witness, come to set right the vision."

"You remember God when distress assaults you; you forget Him when you are free from it. You do not realise that I am everywhere at all times, that God is not confined to the upper regions of the sky or to one little room where you keep his picture! He can be concretised anywhere by sincere prayer. Pray to Him, pointedly, with any Form or Name. He will answer; only, do not change the name and form, as fancy flits; then, concentration will be impposssible. All names are His; all Forms are His; but, when you are striving to concretise Him, it is best to select the Name and Form that appeal to you most."

"Many hesitate to believe that things will improve, that life for all will be happy and full of joy, that the Golden Age will ever recur. Let me assure that this Dharmaswarupa has not come in vain; it will succeed in averting the crisis that has come upon humanity."

"My name and form will soon be found getting established everywhere. They will occupy every inch of the world."

Sathya Sai Baba's message of One God is causing people from different religions to come together. Christians, Hindus, Muslims and Jews claim that they have come to understand more about their own religion since they have come into contact with Sathya Sai Baba. They also say that they now understand that there is only one God. This heartening news comes at a time when communal hatred and religious strife are rampant throughout the world. Edgar Cayce prophesied a revolution in the ideas of religious thought. It seems a silent but powerful global religious revolution has already set in.

ALMIGHTY POWER

The Divine word will give birth to the substance which contains heaven and earth. An occult mystic who will not be from the clergy. Body, soul and spirit having all power. Everything is under his feet just as in his seat in the heaven.

III.2

NOSTRADAMUS

Another Nostradamus prophecy clearly points to the Advent of the Lord. In this prophecy he foresaw that the Lord will take human form because of his will. In this human form God will retain all his powers. He will appear as an occult Mystic but he will not be from the clergy. During his earthly sojourn, all the powers will be under his feet just as in his seat in the Heaven. The word substance here is referred by Nostradamus to the immortal Lord who pervades heaven and earth.

If Sathya Sai Baba is the Messiah or Lord referred to by Nostradamus and other prophets then according to this prophecy Sai Baba must have all the Godly powers at his disposal. All religions ascribe God with the powers of omnipotence, omnipresence and omniscience.

Sathya Sai Baba does perform many miracles day in and day out. These miracles are performed by him physically as well as thousands of miles away, in the homes of many of his devotees, where he is not even physically present. These miracles far surpass those performed by Jesus Christ and Krishna. With a mere wave of his hand he materializes Holy ash, pictures and lockets of himself and other divine personalities, rings made of solid gold-some times studded with precious stones, metal statues of various 'Gods', etc. These miracles are performed by him in front of many people, some times thousands or hundreds of thousands. Yet the act appears to be spontaneous. Thousands of miles away from his physical presence, in India, U.S.A., England, Germany, Australia and many other countries, Holy Ash, Honey, etc. flow from his photographs in the homes of his devotees.

Scientists have no explanation for these miracles. They are wonderstruck when he transcends all known laws of science right in front of them. Many experts have come to defy him, firmly believing that miracles are not possible and have gone back confused. Late N. Kasturi, in his book, *Loving God* writes about one such person:

"......a learned psychiatrist from San Diego, California, U.S.A., Dr. Samuel Sandweiss, M.D. decided to encounter Baba as a scientist 'to study and understand.......to prove that miracles do not exist. In my way of thinking, a belief in miracles grew out of psychological phenomenon such as mass hysteria or group delusion or the ability of someone to wield an uncanny influence over others to the point of altering their perception of reality. I felt that observing Baba in person would give me an idea of what might have happened at the time of Christ to propogate those incredible stories.' These sentences are from page 27 of his book, *Sai Baba, the Holy Man and the Psychiatrist.*

He came and observed Baba, and on page 47 of the same book, unwittingly demonstrating the insufficiency of the very title he has chosen for it, he writes, "Those Bible stories evidently are not symbolic, but true. The divine does become manifest in order to teach, God does appear on earth. There are forces in the Universe, powers of being, that we cannot ever imagine" and, on the same page he exclaims, "Amazing, unbelievable, unthinkable. The most mind-blowing extraordinary experience-as if the most far fetched science fictions were actually seen to be true."

Yet, Dr. Sandweiss is only one of the thousands of doctors and scientists who came to defy and went back convinced. Expert doctors and scientists acknowledge that Sathya Sai Baba knows more than them in the field of their expertise. Let us not forget that Sathya Sai Baba never completed his schooling and has been in public eye since the age of thirteen. He is also reported to speak all languages-native and foreign.

"Not even the biggest scientist can understand Me by means of the categories to which he is accustomed...." says Sathya Sai Baba.

Materialization is only one aspect of Sai Baba miracles. His other miracles include curing patients of incurable diseases like cancer, paralysis, blindness, etc. He has also helped thousands in crisis situations when they were thousands of miles awyay from his physical presence. He brought back to life a Hong Kong businessman, Bhagwandas Daswani, who had died in the intensive care unit of a hospital after suffering a massive heart attack. Few more incidents of resurrection have been reported.

Journalist V.I.K. Sarin, former Special Correspondent, *The Times of India* and author of *India's North East in Flames*, remarks: "Sai Baba miracles are not for any personal profit. He has been performing miracles for more than five decades. If his miracles were not authentic, he could have fooled some people for some time. But it is highly improbable that he could have fooled milions of people all the time."

Sathya Sai Baba miracles are a reality. Their authenticity is beyond the shadow of any doubt. If it was possible to compile all incidents of his miraculous powers, it would fill volumes after volumes. It is safe to say that it would be an impossible task. Each one of his miracles may be titled 'Believe it or not', 'Truth is stranger than fiction', 'Unbelievable Stories', etc. All those who have witnessed his miracles are wonderstruck. Yet those who have benefitted from his miracles, like those who have been cured of incurable diseases and those whose lives he saved in crisis situation, shed tears of joy in gratitude. One is reminded of the miracles performed by Christ and Krishna.

If these miracles occur because of his omnipotence, what about his powers of omnipresence and omniscience? All those, who have had a chance of meeting Sai Baba personally, claim that Baba knows them like an open book. He has recalled and described their past incidents-both trivial and important ones-in vivid detail as if he was right there with them when those incidents occurred, He talks to them about the secret aspirations of their hearts which they may have never disclosed to any one. Nothing is secret with him, they say. Many fear him for they know that he knows everything, He has even described incidents, while talking to people, as they were happening right at that moment, thousands of miles away. All such incidents have been verified.

Yet the most extraordinary power or quality of Sai Baba is his Love-for everyone. Everyone, who has been granted an interview with Sai Baba, claims that he showered abundant Love on them. A personal interview with him is an experience by itself. He makes the person feel as if the Lord has incarnated on earth just for that person.

Dr. Frank G. Baranowski of the Arizona University has explored the recesses of the human body and mind, especially the auras that form the biomagnetic field around the body and reveal when photographed and interpreted, the emotional make-up and predominant features of the urges of the mind. He visited Sai Baba's Whitefield residence in Bangalore in July, 1978. Earlier, he had visited a number of places in the rest of India and taken photographs of a large number of 'Holy Men' through his highly sophisticated Kirilan photographic technique. Addressing the students and teachers, undergoing Spiritual Summer Camp, and illustrating his deductions with the help of colour slides depicting the human aura, Dr. Baranowski decalred, "If ever I can use the phrase that I have seen Love walking on two feet, it is here (pointing towards Sai Baba)."

He added "I have met over a hundred holy men in India. Too many of these holy men are involved with their personal egos. Their auras show mostly their concern for themselves and their institutions. So, they are only a foot broad or perhaps two feet. I am not a devotee (of Sai Baba). I have come here from America as a scientist to see this man, Sai Baba. I saw him on Sunday, standing there on the balcony, giving darshan to the devotees singing below. The aura Swami (Sai Baba) projected was not that of man. The white was more than twice the size of any man's, the blue was practically limitless, and then there was gold and silver bands beyond even those, far beyond this building, right upto the horizon. There is no scientific explanation for this phenomenon. His aura is so strong that it is affecting me, standing by the chair on which he is sitting. I can feel the effect and I have to wipe my arm, off and on, as you may have noticed. I have given over 6,000 lectures in all parts of the world, but for the first time, believe me, my kness are shaking."

Dr. Baranowski further stated, "I was not brought up in any belief, though I am a Christian born and a Roman Catholic. The scientific community in my country finds it difficult to accept a God. It is not scientific, they assert. I am risking my reputation when I make this statement. Two days ago, right outside this hall, I looked into his eyes; they have a glow inside them. It was clear to me that I had looked into the face of Divinity. There is no scientific explanation for this.... In My estimation, he is exactly what he appears to be, what he wants you to be..........LOVE. That is what he is."

Dr. Baranowski says that he has met personalities like President Gerald Ford, Queen Juliana of Netherlands, Pope John Paul II and Queen Elizabeth II of Great Britain. He has examined the auras of these personalities as well as the auras of tens of thousands of others. "I say this not as a testimonial but as a fact, not one person I have ever seen has an aura to compare to the size and colour of Sathya Sai Baba's aura." He adds that the colour blue is an indication of deep spirituality. Baranowski also saw Sathya Sai Baba with the pink aura. Baranowski says that this colour is rarely seen and it typifies a person capable of selfless Love.

Edgar Cayce saw an aura around every person. This was nature's gift to him. Cayce could predict future success or failure of a person on the basis of aura. According to him the colour blue is the colour of the spirit. People with this colour are engaged in selfless causes and are spiritual minded. Dr. Baranowski had seen limitless blue in Sai Baba's aura. White, says Cayce, is the perfect colour signifying perfect balance. As already mentioned Dr. Baranowski saw twice the amount of white in Sai Baba's aura as compared with any other man's. The aura certainly cannot lie.

Dr. Baranowski was granted an interview by Sathya Sai Baba. While in the interview room, he wanted to ask Sai Baba about his grandson, a one year old baby, who was born with heart defect. Even before the doctor could open his mouth Sai Baba told him that the baby would undergo an operation on the day Baranowski returned home in Arizona and that the baby would be well. Baranowski protested that this could not be true as the baby was not old enough to undergo such an operation. The doctors had made it clear that the minimum age for the operation was two or two and a half years. Sai Baba asserted that the baby would be operated upon on the day

Baranowski returned home. Dr. Baranowski says that the baby was operated upon on the day he arrived in Arizona and that the child did survive contrary to the doctor's expectations.

This story is just a drop in the ocean of Sai Baba's powers. "Everything will be under his feet just as in his seat in the heaven" prophesied Nostradamus.

What does Sai Baba say about his miraculous powers? The following relevant excerpts from his discourses may answer our question:

"The power of Sai is limitless. It manifests for ever, all forms of power are resident in this Sai palm......."

"God can do anything he has all power in the palm of His Hand! My powers do not abide in me a while and then fade away!...... My body, like all other bodies, is a temporary habitation, but My Power is eternal, all pervasive, everlasting......"

"......they exaggerate the role of miracles, which are as trivial, when compared to My glory and majesty, as a mosquito is in size and strength to the elephant upon which it squats. Therefore, when you speak about these miracles, I laugh within myself out of pity, that you allow yourself so easily to lose the precious awareness of My Reality.

"My power is immeasurable; My truth is inexplicable, unfathomable......"

"I am determined to correct you only after informing you of My credentials. That is why I am now and then announcing My Nature by means of miracles that is, acts which are beyond human capacity and human understanding. Not that I am anxious to show off My powers. The object is to draw you close to Me, to cement your hearts to Me."

"I know all that happens to all because I am in everyone. This current is in every bulb. I illumine every consciousness. I am the inner motivator in each one of you."

"I am the inner spring in all that moves and exists. I am the energy, the power that propels and impels. I am the knower, the known and the knowledge............ I am always aware of the future, the past as well as the present of every one of you......... I know the agitations of your heart and its aspirations, but you do not know My heart. I react to the pain that you undergo, to the joy that you feel; for I am in every heart. I am the dweller in that temple."

"Yearn for the Love that will bring you the Love of GOD, Prema, Love. I have no power mightier than that. I might change earth into sky or sky into earth, but that power is nothing before the power of Love....... I am the embodiment of Love; Love is My Instrument."

"What I will must take place; What I plan must succeed...Willing is superfluous for Me, for My Grace is ever available to devotees who have steady Love and Faith. Since I move freely among them, talking and singing, even intellectuals are unable to grasp My truth, My Power, My Glory, or My real task as an Avatar. I can solve any problem, however, knotty. I am beyond the reach of the most intensive inquiry and the most meticulous measurement. Only those who have recognised My Love and experienced that Lòve can assert that they have glimpsed My Reality. For, the Path of Love is the Royal Road that leads mankind to Me."

THREE TEMPORAL KINGS

Through the powers of three temporal kings, the holy seat will be shifted to another place. Where the substance and the corporal spirit will be placed and recognised as true seat.

VIII. 99

NOSTRADAMUS

Nostradamus says that the holy seat will be moved to another place because of the powers of three Temporal kings. This will happen when the Lord assumes physical form. The new seat will be recognised as the true seat. The word substance stands for the Immortal Lord. The holy seat is referred to the seat of the pope in Vatican. There are other prophecies suggesting that after the present pope John Paul II there will only be two more popes. The words 'Corporal Spirit' mean that the Immortal Lord will take a physical body.

As mentioned earlier Sathya Sai Baba claims to be the reincarnation of Sai Baba of Shirdi. Many devotees of Shirdi Sai Baba, who had personally known him, have attested to this fact. As proof, they say, Sathya Sai Baba narrated various incidents and specific dialogue which transpired between these devotees and Sai Baba of Shirdi.

Sathya Sai Baba has also said that after he leaves his present body at the age of 95 (around 2020AD) he will reincarnate as Prema Sai Baba in Mandya District of South India. According to him, he will thus complete the Triple Incarnation as promised, thousands of years ago, to sage Bhardwaj by the Supreme personality of Godhead.

Nostradamus made an uncanny prophecy on this triple incarnation. He prophesied that the holy seat will be shifted to another place because of this Triple Incarnation and it will be recognised as true seat in its new place.

Sathya Sai Baba has materialised photographs and lockets showing the still to incarnate Prema Sai Baba.

This Nostradamus prophecy gives us the glimse of near future. It is likely to come to pass around 1998 A.D.

THE GREAT LAW GIVER

The Sacred pomp will come to lower its wings because of the coming of The Great Law Giver. He will raise the humble and plague the rebels. No one like him will ever be born on earth.

V. 79

NOSTRADAMUS

In this Prophecy Nostradamus says that the Sacred Pomp will lower its wings when the Lord comes in human form. He will give the world new and great laws. He will also raise the humble and plague the rebels. The last line needs no clarification. The 'Second Coming' theme is consistent in all these prophecies. Advent of the Lord is described beautifully in the words "Sacred Pomp will come to lower its wings."

Edgar Cayce warned, "The day of the Lord is near at hand." When those that have gradually forgotten God entirely have been eliminated, and there has come, and will come at the close of this next year, the period when there will be no part of the Globe where man has not had the opportunity to hear, 'THE LORD, HE IS GOD', and when this period has been accomplished, the new era, the new age, is to begin." According to all Cayce readings this period is to commence around the year 1998 A.D.

"Times and times and half times are at an end. The righteous shall inherit the earth" warns Cayce. In another statement Cayce adds, "As the spirit of God once moved to bring peace and harmony out of chaos, so must the spirit move over earth and magnify itself in the hearts, minds and soul of men to bring peace, harmony and understanding....."

Many people have ignored these warnings as being confused with the traditional millennium. Yet we find that Sai Baba says, "I shall scorch the wrong doer for his wrong and sooth the virtuous for his righteousness. Justice shall be meted out to all." Should this be considered as a final warning by the Lord himself? We have only few years before the Golden Age commences in 1998. Yet even Sai Baba devotees have taken him for granted. Both Cayce and Nostradamus have warned us that if we do not reform the results will be disastrous. These Prophets are unanimous about the impending disasters. Since prophecies on doom and gloom are outside the scope of this book, we shall not go into these details.

What else is Sai Baba's mission? He says that he has come on a mission to unite the entire mankind and to establish Sanathana Dharma, the Eternal religion. According to Sai Baba:

"......this Sai has come in order to achieve the supreme task of unifying the entire mankind, as one family through the bond of brother-hood of affirming and illumining the Atmic reality of each being in order to reveal the Divine which is the basis on which the entire Cosmos rests and of instructing all to recognise the common Divine Heritage that binds man to man......"

"I have come on a task which I have imposed on myself. That task will go on, from victory to victory, irrespective of praise or blame. It can neither be halted or hindered."

"The success of the task for which I have come will very soon reverberate throughout the world. The truth that all faiths are facets of the One and that all roads lead to the same goal, is provoking to some persons".

What exactly is Sanathana Dharma? Sathya Sai Baba describes it in his own words: "Sanathana Dharma is the only religion that declares that there is no religion that can be labelled 'One and Only'. It says that all religions are but facets of the One Truth, that all Names are names of God, that all forms are but His Form. No religion can claim to represent fully the universal Eternal Truth. This is the teaching of Sanathana Dharma. Therefore, if any one finds fault with another's faith, he is casting a slur on his own faith. If any one defames another religion, he only reveals his ignorance of the nature of religion and the glory of God......."

"Sanathan Dharma is the very basis of living. It deals with the total personality. It embraces all faiths and has established worldwide influence. Sanathana means Eternal. Only a Dharma which can win universal acceptance can be named Sanathana. The religions we know are all derived from a person or prophet who is adored as the ideal. Islam has Mohammed, Christianity has Jesus, Buddhism has the Buddha. But Sanathan Dharma is not derived from or through a person. It is the primal essence of all the messages the prophets proclaimed......

"You can witness very soon the restoration of Sanathana Dharma laid down in the Vedas for the good of all the people of the world."

Edgar Cayce also had the power of Retrocognition-the ability to see past events. In retrocognition, he saw man's history on earth. His readings support the fact that the Law of One God and the Law of Love were the basis of religion when life evolved on earth. ".....the Lord thy God is One and not a house divided against itself", said Cayce. He prophesied revolution in the ideas of religious thought.

In this light let us consider another Nostradamus prophecy. In the previous mentioned prophecy V. 79 Nostradamus foresaw the Advent of the Lord who will give the world great laws. In the next prophecy we find Nostradamus predicting the success of Sai Baba's mission.

Sacred Shrines that were once built in the Roman way will be rejected as broken foundations. They will take back their previous and humane laws, chasing away most of the cults of the saints.

II. 8

NOSTRADAMUS

This prophecy is connected with prophecy VIII.99 discussed earlier. In this particular prophecy Nostradamus foresaw the establishment of Sanathana Dharma which he beautifully describes as 'their early and humane laws'. He also saw people rejecting sacred shrines built in the Roman way. This prophecy may come to pass after 1998 A.D. In prophecy VIII.99 Nostradamus also saw the shifting of 'Holy Seat'. Please also refer to Prophecy 1.96 mentioned in the next chapter. These three prophecies are very closely related. In prophecy 111.4 and 111.95 (not mentioned in this book) Nostradamus also foresees the downfall of other religions.

ORNATE SPEECHES

The one who will be responsible for destroying the shrines and sects, which have changed out of sheer fancy or caprice, will come to harm more the rocks than the living beings. His ornate speeches everybody will be willing to hear.

1.96

NOSTRADAMUS

In the previous mentioned prophecy 11.8 Nostradamus foresaw people destroying shrines and sects. In this prophecy, he gives more reasons for it. He says that shrines and sects would deviate from the path for which they were originally built and formed. This does, by and large, describe the present state of affairs of all major religions and their establishments. In this prophecy he also foresaw that all will be willing to hear the ornate speeches of the One who will be responsible for the destruction of shrines and sects. This Entity will harm more the rocks rather than the living beings. Rocks, here stand for temples and sects. Nostradamus implies that this man will be more concerned about the living beings.

Sathya Sai Baba says that there is only One God and He is Omnipotent and Omniscient. "Whom the Muslims adore as Allah, the Christians as Jehovah, the Vaishnavas as Phullabjaaksha and the Saivaites as Sambhu, who grants, in answer to their several prayers health, prosperity and happiness to all, wheverever they may be, He, the One God, is the God of all mankind. The followers of every religion, in their own way and style, call upon the One God who is Omnipresent. No religion has a separate God showering Grace upon those who profess to abide by that faith alone! The cause of the illness and of misery is in your mental vision, for, you see many, when there is only One. You say 'My God', 'Their God', 'Your Baba', as if there are so many Gods existing to help you quarrel and fight among yourselves."

When all religions proclaim that God is all pervading and omnipresent then it is logical to infer that there can be only One God. Cayce readings say that the Law of One God was the basis on which the earlier religions evolved. The readings also say that God is all pervading and the beginning and the end of everything.

Sathya Sai Baba says that God is Love and Love is the way to God. Of course, he refers to selfless love rather than selfish love. Cayce readings suggest that Law of Love and equality will be the basis on which the new world order will arise around the year 1998 A.D. Sai Baba says: "You talk of International Understanding, but it can come only when the idea of difference and separateness inherent in the world nations, disappears and when man sees the Lord in all men. God is in the heart of every being and so, one has to love another as one loves God."

What does Sai Baba stand for? What is his message? To answer these questions, we must consider some excerpts from his various discourses:

God is Omnipotent, Omnipresent and Omniscient

"God is All. He is all Forms, His is all Names. There is no place where He is not; no moment when He is not!"

"The Lord is the unseen foundation on which your life is built. He is the source, sustenance and strength. Without His will, no leaf can turn, no blade of grass can quiver. What firmer foundation can you desire than this? Once you know that the Lord, the Omnipotent Power, is the mainspring of your life, there will be no fear any more."

"God is Eternal power, Omnipotent and Omniscient. He is the Cause and Consequence, the Potter, the Clay and the Pot. Without God, there can be no Universe. He willed and the Universe happened. It is His Play, the Manifestation of His Power. Man embodies His will, His power, His wisdom. But, he is unaware of this glory. A cloud of ignorance veils the truth. God sends sages, saints and prophets to unveil the Truth and Himself appears as an Avatar to awaken and liberate him."

"The Lord is neither in Heaven, nor in Kailash or in Vaikunth or Swarg. To believe that He is manifest only in one place or location and to journey thither is a superstition much to be deplored. He is everywhere, in every one, at all times. He is the Witness of all, in all. He is the energy that fills space and time and He is the energy that manifests as causation."

"When the Cosmos manifested through the Will of God, Who is the Universal Absolute, it arose from the Absolute. Only, since there was then, only ONE, just as even now there is only One, in spite of all this seeming variety. That Will which emanated from the Absolute persuaded us to see and experience Many; that is all that has happened. The One Reality is still the One, it has not undergone any change. We have super-imposed on the One, the illusion of the Many!"

"God, therefore, is the material cause as well as the instrumental cause, the gold and the goldsmith, the potter and the clay, the seed as well as the tree."

"God is all-pervading; but, yet, we have some scientists who assert, "We have searched all outer space, we have looked for Him on the Moon; no; He is Nowhere to be found. He does not exist. They do not know what to seek and where; still; they have the impudence to assert that it is not found. Is God an occupant of an identifiable body or Form, has He a habitation and a habiliment that is traditionally His? God is all this and more. He is in all this and beyond. He is the inner motivator of the very scientist who 'denies' Him! Man himself is God; all matter even in the Moon, is suffused with the Divine Presence. To search for God with the instruments of the laboratory is like trying to cure pain in the stomach by pouring drops into the eye! There is technique and a special instrument for that purpose, which the pastmasters in that science have developed and spoken about. Equip yourselves with a clear eye, through detachment and love, sharpen your sense of discrimination, Viveka, so that it has no prejudice or predilection, then, you can see God in you, around you, in all that you know and feel and are. The doctor asks you to remove your shrit before he applies the stethoscope and tries to diagnose your illness. You have another shirt covering your chest, the desires that surge in your heart. I remove that shirt, so that your real nature, that is Divinity, can be revealed, to you and all who seek to know you."

"Man extols God as omnipresent, omniscient and omnipotent, but he ignores His Presence in himself! Of course many venture to describe the attributes of God and proclaim Him to be such and such; but, these are but their own guesses and the reflections of their own predilection and preferences."

"Who can affirm that God is this or thus? Who can affirm that God is not of this form or with this attribute? Each one can acquire from the vast expanse of the ocean only as much as can be contained in the vessel he carries to its shore. From that quantity, they can grasp but little of that immensity."

BASIS OF ALL RELIGIONS

"God is omnipresent; He is the Inner Motivator of every particle in the Universe. To declare that He is amenable only to your style of worhip, that He will answer only to the Name that you have learnt to use, is to insult His Omniscience and His Glory. See Him in all, serve Him in all. Pray, 'Let the whole world prosper; let all mankind be happy.'

"All men in all countries are pilgrims proceeding along the path to God. The progress of each is decided by the discipline adopted, the character formed, the ideal kept in view, the leadership chosen and the faith implanted. Just as trees and plants, birds and beasts differ from one region to another, the rituals, practices, disciplines and ideals may differ from community to comunity; each is good for that region and that stage of development. You cannot transplant one, from one human community to another. The atmosphere in which you have grown up is the most congenial for you."

The process of splitting into diverse viewpoints has taken place in all the major religions. Islam has the Shia and Sunni sects; Christianity has Catholics and Protestants. But however deep the cleavage, no sect denies God and no sect extols violence and falsehood. Names may be different, the facets emphasised may be different, but the Almighty Providence is denoted as Absolute and Eternal. The terminology may be different but the concept is not different. God may be referred to as Allah, prayer may be called namaz, priests may be known as kajis, scholars may be hailed as mullahs, the Bible may be in the form of the Holy Quran. But the undercurrent of energising power in all cases is Love, Love of all beings towards all beings. The founders had always in view the Unity of all life and the progressive march of man from mere humanness to the heights of Divinity."

"Form of worship, the phraseology of adoration or the style of address may vary; but, all religions are directed towards the same consummation. The same bloodstream circulates in all limbs of the body. The same divine stream activates the entire Universe. Visualise that supreme Architect, that incomprehensible Designer, that unseen Lifegiver. This is spoken of as the realisation of the Fatherhood of God and the Brotherhood of Men. Do not get entangled in the business of living; do not forget in your struggle for survival and success the God that made life possible."

"Each religion defines God within the limits it demarcates and then claims to have grasped Him. Like the seven blind man who spoke of the elephant as a pillar, a fan, a rope or a wall, because they contacted but a part and could not comprehend the entire animal, so too, religions speak of a part and assert that its vision is full and total."

"Each religion forgets that God is all Forms and all Names, all attributes and all assertions. The Religion of Humanity is the sum and substance of all these partial faiths; for, there is only one Religion and that is the Religion of Love. The various limbs of the elephant that seemed separate and distinct to the eye-less seekers of its truth were all fostered and activated by one single stream of blood; the various religions and faiths that feel separate and distinct are all fostered by one single stream of Love."

"Love for the Lord should not degenerate into fanaticism and hatred of other names and forms. This type of cancer is affecting even eminent men, nowadays. But you must avoid it. Believe that all who revere the Lord and walk in fear of sin are your brothers, your nearest kith and kin. Their outer dress or language or skin-colour, or even the methods they adopt to express their reverence and fear are not important at all. Sugar dolls are valued for the sugar, not the shapes they are given by the manufacturer. Their sweetness makes men purchase them an elephant, a dog, a cat, a rat, a jackal or a lion- it does not matter. That is a matter of individual fancy. Each is sweet, that is the essential thing. The sweetness draws the manava towards Madhava; the pravriththi (deed) towards nivriththi (dedication), the Ananda (joy) towards Sath-chith-ananda (Highest Bliss). When the appetite for these grows, all low desires and hungers cease."

"Religions attempt to implant holy ideals in the heart of man but man does not allow them to sprout and grow. His egoistic craving for power and competitive success has, in most cases, persuaded him to use religion as an instrument of torture and persecution. Instead of uniting mankind in a common endeavour, it has become a system of walled enclosures, guarded by hate and fanaticism. So each religion is an armed camp sunk in self-aggrandizement, trying to wean others into itself and preventing defections from itself. Religion, therefore, is being condemned as the root of chaos and conflict. In spite of great progress in many other areas of life, religious animosity is aflame even today in many many parts of the world."

"It has to be emphasised that religion is not the root cause of this state of affairs. The factional fights and fanatic hatred are due to the unruly ego that is given free play. Religion strives to destroy just this vicious tendency, so it has to be supported, not condemned. What has to be condemned is the narrow, perverted attitude of hating those who do not agree with you or who hold different opinions of the Mysterious Force that animates the universe. Religious wars and conflicts breed in the slime of ignorance and avarice. When people are blind to the truth that the human family is one indivisible Unity, they grope in the dark and are afraid of strange touch. The cultivation of love alone can convince man of this truth that there is only one caste-the caste of Humanity, and only one religion-the religion of Love. Since no religion upholds violence or despises love, it is wrong to ascribe the chaos to religion."

"It is also not advisable to engage in campaigns of vilification or exaggerated propagation of any religion with a view to drawing votaries. If only each one lives up to the ideals propounded by the founders of one's religion, unaffected by greed or hate, the world will be a happier and more peaceful habitation for man."

GOD IS LOVE

"Start the Day with Love; Spend the Day with Love; Fill the Day with Love; End the Day with Love; That is the way to God."

"Love alone can reveal the Divinity latent in all. Love is God. Live in Love. Love lives by giving and forgiving; Self lives by getting and forgetting. Love is self-lessness; Selfishness is love-lessness. Do not waste your life pursuing the narrow interests of the self. Love! Love! Become what you truly are, the embodiments of Love. No matter how others treat you or what they think of you, do not worry. Follow Jesus Christ. Love for your own evolution and not for what others say. Do not imitate others. Cultivate your own life. You have your own heart, your own opinion, your ideas, your own will. Why then imitate? Imitation is human, they say; but Creation is Divine. Follow your chosen path. Let your own experience of God be your guide and master. Do not go into the grave, weakly copying others. You won't find God if you search in the outside world. Your own heart shining with Love is God's Love. Follow the Master. Face the Devil, Fight to the end and Finish the game.

"You are God. The true you is God.

"Love all beings-that is enough. Love with no expectation of return; love for the sake of love because your very nature is Love. Love because that is the form of Worship you know and like.

"Cultivate Love; share that love with all. How can you give one person less and another more when they are both the same as you? If you forget the basic Divinity, hatred sprouts: envy raises its hood."

"I have come to light the Lamp of Love in your hearts, to see that it shines day by day with added lustre. I have not come to speak on behalf of any particular Dharma, like the Hindu Dharma. I have not come on any mission of publicity for any sect or creed or cause; nor have I come to collect followers for any doctrine. I have no plan to attract disciples or devotees into My fold or any fold. I have come to tell you of this Universal unitary faith, this Atmic principle, this Path of Love, this Dharma of Prema, this duty of Love, this obligation to Love."

"God is the source of all Love; Love God, Love the world as the gesture of God, no more, no less. Through Love, you can merge in the Ocean of Love. Love cures pettiness, hate and grief.

Love loosens bonds; it saves man from the torment of birth and death. Love binds all hearts in a soft silken symphony. Seen through the eyes of love, all beings are beautiful, all deeds are dedicated, all thoughts are innocent. The world is one vast kin."

"God is everywhere. He is everything; so, it appears as if He is nowhere and He is not in anything! For to know Him you have to identify Him as someone foreign and something unique. We forget that everything is foreign to us, everything has a uniqueness of its own! On what authority can you deny? On what authority do you accept? You cannot deny Love, or Truth or Wisdom. He is Love, Power, Truth, Wisdom, Beauty. When you accept Love, you accept God. The tender plant of spirituality can grow only in the field of Love. It cannot thrive in the dehydrated loveless land of human hearts."

Love is of three kinds: Swaartha or self-centred, which like a bulb, illumines just a small room; Anyonya or mutual, which like the moonlight spreads wider but is not clearer; and Paraartha or other-centred, which like the sunlight is all pervasive and clear. Cultivate the third type of love; that will save you. For all the service that you do to others through that love is in fact service done to yourself. It is not the others that you help, it is yourself that is helped, remember.

"Love....Love....Love.... First...Love, as along as life lasts. For myself, I can say, I shower more blessings on those who decry or defame me than those who worship and adore me! For, those who spread falsehoods about me derive joy therefrom; I am happy that I am the cause for their exultation and joy. You too must accept this line of argument and be very happy when someone derives joy by defaming you. Do not respond by defaming that person; then, the chain of hatred will bind both and drag both down. Life will become a tragedy. Conquer anger by means of fortitude; conquer hatred by love. Do not feed anger with retaliation; do not feed hatred with fury.

"Foster Love. Live in Love, spread Love-that is the spiritual exercise which will yield the maximum benefit. When you recite the Name of God, remembering all the while His Majesty, His Compassion, His Glory, His Splendour, His Presence, Love will grow within you, its roots will go deeper, and deeper, its branches will spread wider and wider giving cool shelter to friend and foe, to fellow national and foreigner.

"God is love; so, all things created by God are filled with love. A silver cup is all silver, it is silver with an identifiable name and form. The Cosmos has a name and form; God became the Cosmos; God is love and so the cosmos is Love. From the silver cup, you can never separate the silver as a distinct entity. So too, God cannot be distinct from Creation. Nothing is mean or low, ugly or disgusting; every thing is adorable. To get fixed in this universal God consciousness, one has to tame one's impulses and educate one's desires.

"Names and forms are different naturally; but they are all aspects of the ONE. Love must bind all believers together; not only belivers but non-believers too must be loved and served as His images.

"Love must be manifested as Service, Seva. Seva must take the form of food for the hungry, solace for the forlorn, consolation for the sick and the suffering. Jesus wore himself out in such Seva. The Heart full of Compassion is the temple of God. Jesus pleaded for Compassion. Compassion was His Message. He was sorely distressed at the sight of the poor. This day Jesus is worshipped but His teachings are neglected. Sai is being worshipped but His teaching are neglected. Everywhere, pomp, pageantry, hollow exhibitionism! Lectures! Lectures! Lectures! No activity, no love, no seva. Heroes while lecturing, zeroes while putting what is said in to practice.

"God has incarnated in human form, in order to inspire man to follow higher ideals not only in India but foreign countries also. Men may have different languages and life styles but God is One and He is present everywhere. All religions speak of him as Love and as attainable through Love. Forms of worshipping God differ, for they are shaped by time and place but Love is the basic content of all the forms. The language of Love is understood and spoken by all hearts. There is only one race really, and that is the race of mankind.

We now consider petty distinctions of nationality, race, religion and language as vital and hold back Love which must flow to every one from the heart. That was the life and message of Jesus. Nurture it in your hearts. Experience Jesus as your Messenger sent from God.

"Jesus was Love. Sathya Sai too is Love. That explains the gathering of Christians of all sects, which we see here. In Rome today, Catholics gather to celebrate the Advent of Jesus. The Protestants celebrate it by themselves in their churches. The Jews are not welcomed anywhere. But in the presence of Sathya Sai, all are equally welcome. The Jews arraingned Jesus and demanded that he should be punished; in this Presence, Jews are adoring that very Jesus. The Prema of Sathya Sai has transformed and transcended those memories, it has made them realise that there is only one caste, the Caste of Humanity, there is only one religion, the Religion of Love.

"Of course, I love all: those who come to Me as well as those who stop coming: those who stay at the Nilayam, as well as those who stay away, those who praise, as well as those who blame. For no one is beyond the boundary of My Love.

INHERENT DIVINITY OF MAN

"All men are caskets containing Divine Glory.

"All Energy, Power and Intelligence are in you; you need not search for them outside yourselves. God who is manifesting as Time, Space and Causation is in you; why then do you feel weak and helpless?

"Every individual is a spark of the effulgence of God; God is dancing in every cell of every being. Do not doubt this, or ignore this, or dispute this. This is the Truth; this is the entire Truth; this is the only Truth. The Universe is God, Loka is Lokesa, All this is He, His Body.

"Man has in him all the Bliss, as well as all the equipment needed to unravel it; but, he is caught in dire ignorance of his own inner resources. He can have Supreme Peace but, he does not strive to earn it; his attempts are weakened by doubt and indecision, and so, they are doomed to failure, Of course, there is the flow of water underneath the ground. But, how can we benefit by it unless efforts are made to dig down into that source? A good deal of Desire for-sense-satisfaction has to be removed before that inner Spring of Peace and joy can be tapped.

"Your lives are essentially of the nature of Peace(Santhi), your Nature is essentially Love; your hearts are saturated with Truth. Rid yourselves of the impediments that prevent their manifestation: You do not make any attempt towards this and so, there is no Peace or Love or Truth in the home, the community, the nation and the world.

"Sin is not the real nature of man; it is acquired and can be shed. Man is pure, good, loving, wise. That is why in the Nilayam, I have stopped people from reciting slokas which proclaim man as sinful, born in sin, revelling in sin etc. Let the purity, which you are, get manifested; endeavour to express it in your activities; that is what pleases me and wins my Grace.

"Man is inherently Divine; he ought therefore to demonstrate in thought, word and deed the Divine attributes of Love, Tolerance, Compassion and Humanity. God is Truth; man too must live in Truth. God is Love; man too must live in Love, eschewing Anger. Master hatred through Love; master anger through sweet Tolerance.

Man is Divinity humanised; in him is concentrated vast power, awaiting manifestation. But, man condemns himself into poverty, disease and despair. He begs for alms from all and sundry and debases the Lord within. He tells himself that God is far away, in an unreachable Heaven. He exiles himself from the Kingdom which is his legitimate heritage. He deludes himself into the belief that it is he who feels, thinks, speaks, and acts. He curses himself as a fool or as a victim of fate, commiting wrong with every such imprecation! Examine each of you, your own minds and avoid this cowardice which denies your birthright.

People have lost the comfort of self-reliance; they have no faith in their own strength, and no confidence in others. Man is the most devalued entity today; everything else has risen in value; man is cheap; he can be neglected with impunity. He knows not his own greatness or worth. He does not know how to elevate the smallest act of his into a means of realising the Grace of the Lord. He does not know the alchemy by which every failure or disappointment can be transmuted into a golden chance for self-surrender and for building up the bulwark or Bhakthi. He fritters away precious time in paltry activities and petty pleasures, which lower his self-respect and injure his physical and mental calibre.

"It is not possible to consider creation and the creator, Nature and God as different or separate. Can we say that waves are separate from the sea? They are of the sea, with the sea and from the sea. Man too is of God, with and from God. The bubble is born in water, stays in water and is lost in water as water. The Cosmos too is a bubble born in the Absolute, exists as the Absolute and merges in the Absolute or Paramatma. Nara (the human) is the bubble:God(Narayana) is the sea. Recognise this truth:as the bubble cannot be conceived as without God. Of course waves rise and fall, advance and recede, but the sea has no such agitations. The movements of the waves do not affect the sea. As a consequence of human activities, man has ups and downs in life, growth and decay. But the God in him is not affected at all.

"Once a person came to Me and argued that there was no God and he was not prepared to believe in one. Well, I asked him, 'Have you faith atleast in yourself? Which is your self? Your self is God. You have faith in your judgement, your intelligence, your ability, because God within you tells you not to falter or fear. That assurance wells from within, from your basic Truth, which is otherwise called God. It does not matter if you do not call it God; it is enough if you believe in Yourself; that is the real test of theism,' I told him.

"I say the same thing to you also. The body is the temple of God; in every body, God is installed, whether the owner of the body recognises it or not. It is God that inspires you to do good acts that warns you against the bad. Listen to that Voice. Obey that Voice and you will not come to any harm.

"Remember that with every step, you are nearing God, and God too, when you take one step towards Him takes ten towards you. There is no stopping place in this pilgrimage, it is one continuous journey, through day and night; through valley and desert; through tears and smiles, through death and birth, through tomb and womb. When the road ends, and the goal is gained, the pilgrim finds that he has travelled only from himself to himself, that the way was long and lonesome, the God that led him upto it was all the while in him, around him, with him and beside him! He always was divine. His yearning to merge within God was but the sea calling to the Ocean! Man Loves, because he is Love! He creaves for melody and harmony, because he is melody and harmony. He seeks joy, for, he is joy, He thirsts for God, for he is composed of God, and he cannot exist without him.

REVERE MAN, REVERE GOD

"Believe that God resides in all beings; speak such words as would spread goodness, truth and beauty; do such acts as would promote the happiness and prosperity of all; pray that all words have Peace. Expand yourselves; do not contract into your own tiny individuality. Expand into Universal Love, unshaken equanimity, and ever-active virtue. That is the Path which will bring out the Divinity in you to the fullest.

"This temple is but brick and mortar. This idol is but stone. But, you are determined to see in it the Divine Principle. If you can penetrate behind the stone and see the Divine Basis, how much easier it is to see the Lord who resides in the heart of every living, every human being? Try to realise that first, so that your faith in this idol and this temple can be well settled. Revere Man; that is the first step towards reverence for God; for, Man is Prathyaksha. God is Paroksha. Man is perceptible; God is imperceptible.

"The service of man is more valuable than what you call "service to God". God has no need of your service. Please man; you please God.

"Devotion should not be confined to the four walls of the shrine-room, or the few minutes you perform Dhyana. It is a fulltime Sadhana. Your devotion has to be expressed as worship of every one, as a living embodiment of Divinity. See God in every one, even in persons whom you regard as your enemies. Practice that broad inclusive type of Love. How can you derive happiness by showing love and reverence to a stone idol; that does not respond or reflect the feeling? Living beings will return appreciation and gratitude and wish you well. You can see joy growing in their faces. That will confer satisfaction on you. If you cannot educate yourself to love your fellowman, how can you follow the path of dedication to God?

"Man is mortal; dust he is and to dust returneth. But, in him, there shines Atma, as a Spark of the Immortal Flame. This is not a term of flattery invented by the Vedantists. The Atma is the source, the sustenance of every being and every organisation of beings. It is the one and only Source, Substance and Sustenance. The Atma is God; the Particular is the Universal, no less. Therefore, recognise in each being, in each man, a brother, the child of God, and ignore all limiting thoughts and prejudices based on status, colour, class, nativity and caste. Sai is ever engaged in warning you and guiding you so that you may think, speak and act in this attitude of Love."

Golden Rules

"There is only one God; He is omnipresent. There is only one religion, the Religion of Love; there is only one caste, the Caste of Humanity; there is only one language, the Language of the Heart."

"Develop compassion. Live in Love. Be Good; Do Good and See Good. This is the way to God."

"Idea, principles, laws, customs, codes, habits, actions all are to be judged on the twin points of intention and consequence. Is the intention pure, is it born out of Prema, is it based on Truth? Does it result in Santhi?"

"Consider all your acts as Worship. Duty is God; Work is Worship. Whatever happens accept it gladly as His Handiwork, a sign of His Compassion."

"Bring something into your daily practice, as evidence of your having known the secret of the higher life from Me. Show that you have greater brotherliness, speak less, with more sweetness and self-control, that you can bear defeat as well as victory with calm resignation."

"Of what avail is it if you simply worship My Name and Form, without attempting to cultivate the Samathwa (love for all) that I have, My Santhi (unruffled equanimity) My Prema (Love), My Sahana (Patience and Fortitude), My Ananda (Ever-blissful Nature)"?

"I declare that I am in every one, in every being. So do not hate any one, or cavil at any one. Spread Prema always, everywhere. That is the best way of revering Me. Do not seek to measure Me or evaluate Me. I am beyond your understanding. Pray or worship for your own satisfaction and contentment. But to say that I will respond only if I am called or that I will save only if I am thought of is wrong".

"You must realise by constant contemplation that the world is the Body of God. And, you are a cell, in that Body. The prosperity of the world is your prosperity; feel so, act in that spirit; think in those terms. That is real spirituality".

"Your material eyes see countries as different; in reality all countries are limbs of one organism; all bodies are activated by the same Principle. For God, the universe is the mansion. Each nation is a room, a hall, in that mansion".

"Sai does not live in structures of stone or brick and mortar! He lives in soft hearts, warm with sympathy and fragrant with universal Love".

"God is inscrutable. He cannot be realised in the outer objective world; He is in the very heart of every being. Gemstones have to be sought deep underground; they do not float in mid-air. Seek God in the depths of yourself, not in tantalising, kaleidoscopic Nature. The body is granted to you for this high purpose; but, you are now misusing it".

"One common definition of Dharma is that it is the adherence to the rule: 'Do unto others what you wish them to do unto you; do not do unto others what you do not wish them to do unto you.' Do not have a double standard. Treat all as your own self. That is to say, you must have faith in yourself and then only can you have faith in others. You must respect yourself and respect others. Egoism is the measure at altruism. Mankind is one community; you harm yourself and you harm all. You make a man stand erect and that act makes you stand erect. The treatment you wish others to render to you is itself the measure of your duty to them".

"Like a lighted lamp, God's Grace spreads all round, on all who approach Him and love to be near him; but if you interpose a shade which shuts out the light from you, you have only yourself to blame if Grace does not shine. Open the doors of your heart, so that the Sun may shine through and disinfect the vices therein and illumine its corners. You must initiate that little effort, at least. The Sun will not open the doors and enter. To get the programme right and pleasant, you have to switch on and tune in the receiver. That is an inescapable effort".

"Treat mercifully those who struggle to survive; help them as much as you can; realise your responsibilities; move reverentially with others; win the blessings of Sai and earn good fame among fellow men; examine your daily activities on the touchstone of righteousness; may you become individuals shining in virtue."

"You may have only a picture of Sai Baba before you, or an image in metal or an idol in stone. But, if you have the faith that He is alive and present in it, and that He is in your heart and the hearts of all beings then, you can get the ecstasy of that knowledge, the knowledge that He is omnipresent, omniscient and omnipotent".

THE LAST WORD

Sathya Sai Baba's message that there is only One God and that man is inherently Divine does make a lot of sense. If all religions claim that God is all prevading, Omnipotent and Omniscient, it is logical to infer that there can only be one God. His message, that we must love one another irrespective of geographical, racial, caste or religious differences, can only promote world peace and international cooperation. The fact is that boundaries only exist in our minds. There is no physical demarcation of countries on the planet. Similarly, prejudice against a race or religion is only our personal belief. There is no rational basis behind it. Lack of understanding and information is the main reason for such beliefs.

Many of us might still say that we do not believe Sathya Sai Baba is God. Let's pose a question to ourselves. Do we believe in the Divinity of Rama, Krishna, Jesus, Mohammed, Nanak or Buddha? There are only two possible answers to this question. Let us say that our answer is in the affirmative. In that case what is the reason for this belief? Is there a so called 'scientific evidence' supporting their belief? Well, of-course not. Any evidence supporting their Divinity is not only 'hearsay' but at least few hundred or thousands of years old. Then on what basis do we accept any or all of these personalities as Divine? On the other hand we can say that none of these personalities were divine. We also may say that we do not believe in the existence of God. Why? Is it scientific or rational to judge an issue or theory without going into the details? A scientist first postulates a theory, then experiments and only then does he reach a conclusion. No scientist can deny or accept any theory without following this procedure. It is then logical to infer that if we believe that God does not exist it is our own personal belief and this belief has no scientific or rational basis.

Spiritual scientists have postulated theories on the existence of God. They have experimented with the ways to realise God. All of them have reached the conclusion that God exists. Many saints and sages of various religions, like Ramakrishna Paramhansa and Yogananda, are examples. If we deny their theories and findings without experimenting on the theories they postulated and concluded, our denial is not only unscientific but illogical.

Do we believe that energy exists? Well! of course we do. Why? Well, because scientists have made experiments, reached conclusions and proved that various forms of energy exist. Yes! but did we conduct our own experiments to reach a conclusion? The answer is, No! Not only this but can we see energy or touch it? So, we are taking scientists' word for it. It is true that we can feel some forms of energy but that is as far as we can go. Spiritual scientists, have concluded that God exists and although we may not be able to see God but we can experience God. So, why don't we believe them? Why is a scientific theory more credible than a spiritual theory. As far as we are concerned the evidence supporting a scientific or spiritual theory is hearsay because we have not experimented to reach a conclusion. Just as we cannot negate a scientific theory because of our beliefs, in the same way we cannot negate a spiritual theory because of our beliefs. If we want to reach a scientific conclusion whether God exists or not, we must follow the path shown by spiritual scientists, experiment under 'optimum conditions' and only then we can reach a conclusion. Just as we cannot negate a scientific theory without following this procedure, same way we cannot deny the existence of God without following this procedure. The only other alternative is to accept the theories of other scientists. Any other conclusion is not only our own personal opinion but it is unscientific and irrational.

Many scientists, journalists and editors have demanded that Sai Baba should perform specific miracles under 'controlled conditions." This request has been denied. It seems that there are valid reasons for it. Even if he does grant some of these requests, there would be an unending queue of people demanding that they should also be allowed to examine. Another reason is that most of these people are prejudiced. The precondition of any scientific or rational inquiry is that the person investigating must have an open mind. Contempt and prejudice stems from ignorance. Yet, even before we go that far, these critics must answer a valid question. How much do these scientists and journalists know about God, spirituality or the paranormal phenomenon? On what basis can they sit in judgement over an issue about which their own knowledge is so shallow? One wonders if such people would have liked to subject Christ and Krishna to such experiments.

Rev. Canon John Rossner, Ph.D., an Anglican priest and Professor in the Concordia University of Canada, describes Sathya Sai Baba as a universal man who embodies the One God. Swami Sivananda personally invited and received Sathya Sai Baba at his Ashram. Sati Mata, an enlightened saint of Rajasthan having an enormous following, acknowledged that Sathya Sai Baba is the supreme personality of Godhead. Sati Mata's enlightenment is unquestionable. She had not eaten or had a drop of water for more than three decades. Doctors have attested to this fact. Are all these personalities gullible?

Sathya Sai Baba is the eternal mirror come to show us our true reality. He says "My life is my message." The world needs his message more than ever before.

According to all prophecies and predictions Sathya Sai Baba is going to emerge as the universal Messiah and savior by the end of this decade. All prophecies and predictions also point to great upheavals on the economic, geographic and political fronts by 2000 A.D. Recent changes in Russia and eastern Europe are evident examples, but these are pleasant changes. According to Edgar Cayce retrocognitive readings, science and technology was more advanced during the Atlantis civilization than our present day technology. People at that time ignored God and His Laws which resulted in the destruction and submerging of the Atlantis.

Are we heading towards the same fiasco? Prophecies on doom and gloom are outside the scope of this book. These may be dealt with in a future book.

It is beyond the shadow of any doubt that Sathya Sai Baba is the Krishna Incarnate referred to by Saint Aurobindo. He is the Messiah predicted by Edgar Cayce, the Lord whose advent and mission Nostradamus prophesied beautifully and the religious leader promised by Madan.

GLOSSARY

Anand	:	Bliss
Atma	:	Soul
Atmic	:	Pertaining to Soul
Avatar, Avathar, Avatara	:	Descent of God in human form
Bhakthi	:	Devotion
Chith	:	All things with life force (no exact English equivalent)
Dharma	:	Religion, Also righteousness or righteous duty
Dharmaswarupa	:	Embodiment of righteousness.
Guru	:	Teacher or Preceptor
Loka	:	World or Universe
Lokesha	:	God or Master of the Universe
Madhava	:	A name for the supreme personality of Godhead
Manava	:	Human being
Maya	:	Delusion
Nilayam	:	Short form of Prasanthinilayam, the residence of Sathya Sai Baba.
Prema	:	Love
Santhi	:	Peace or Bliss
Seva	:	Service
Sri	:	Prefix before male names, like Mr. in English
Viveka	:	Wisdom or power of discrimination
Yuga	:	Age.

OUR PUBLICATIONS

01. A COMPENDIUM OF THE TEACHINGS OF SATHYA SAI BABA (Second Edition)	- Charlene Leslie-Chadan	Rs.555
02. A JOURNEY TO LOVE (Fourth Edition)	- David Bailey	Rs.180
03. A JOURNEY TO LOVE BOOK II LOVE & MARRIAGE	- David Bailey	Rs.275
04. A JOURNEY TO LOVE (Spanish)	- David Bailey	Rs.375
05. A JOURNEY TO LOVE (Telugu)	- David Bailey	Rs. 60
06. "ALEX" THE DOLPHIN	- Light Strom	Rs. 90
07. ANOTHER JOURNEY TO LOVE	- Faye Bailey	Rs.350
08. ASHES, ASHES WE ALL FALL DOWN	- Gloria St. John	Rs. 80
09. A STORY OF INDIA AND PATAL BHUVANESWAR	- Jennifer Warren	Rs. 60
10. AT THE FEET OF SAI	- R. Lowenberg	Rs.120
11. BAPU TO BABA	- V.K. Narasimhan	Rs.120
12. BHAGAVAN SRI SATHYA SAI BABA DISCOURSES IN KODAIKANAL, APRIL 96	- Pooja Kapahi	Rs.120
13. BUDO-KA-TRUE SPIRITUAL WARRIORS	- Deena Naidu	Rs.200
14. CRICKET FOR LOVE - A Souvenir on Sri Sathya Sai Unity Cup		Rs.250
15. CUTTING THE TIES THAT BIND	- Phyllis Krystal	Rs.110
16. CUTTING MORE TIES THAT BIND	- Phyllis Krystal	Rs.120
17. CUTTING THE TIES THAT BIND - WORK BOOK	- Phyllis Krystal	Rs.140
18. DA PUTTAPARTHI A PATAL BHUVANESHWAR (Italian)	- Sandra Percy	Rs.150
19. DEATHING (Indian Edition)	- Anya Foos-Graber	Rs.195
20. DISCOVERING MARTIAL ARTS	- Deena Naidu	Rs.265
21. EDUCATION IN HUMAN VALUES (3 Vols.)	- June Auton	Rs.750
22. FACE TO FACE WITH GOD	- V. I. K. Sarin	Rs.150
23. GLIMPSES OF THE DIVINE	- Birgitte Rodriguez	Rs.150
24. GLORY OF SAI PADHUKAS	- Sai Towers	Rs.100
25. GOD AND HIS GOSPEL	- Dr. M.N.Rao	Rs.120
26. GOD LIVES IN INDIA	- R. K. Karanjia	Rs. 75
27. GOOD CHANCES (Second Edition)	- Howard Levin	Rs.120
28. HANDBOOK FOR SAI TEACHERS - The Sathya Sai Human Values Program	- Dr. R.Farmer & S.Farmer	Rs.560
29. HEART TO HEART (Reprint)	- Howard Levin	Rs.120
30. HOLY MISSION DIVINE VISION	- Sai Usha	Rs. 80
31. IN QUEST OF GOD	- P.P. Arya	Rs.120
32. KNOW THYSELF (Second Edition)	- Gerard T. Satvic	Rs.180
33. LET ME SOW LOVE	- Doris May Gibson	Rs.120
34. LETTERS FROM A GRANDFATHER	- S. K. Bose	Rs.180
35. MESSAGES (Japanese)	- Dr. M.N. Rao	Rs.150
36. MESSAGES FROM MY DEAREST FRIEND SAI BABA	- Elvie Bailey	Rs.130
37. MIRACLES ARE MY VISITING CARDS	- Erlendur Haraldsson	Rs. 180
38. MOHANA BALA SAI (Children's Book)	- Sai Mira	Rs.120
39. MUKTI THE LION FINDS HIMSELF	- Gina Suritsch	Rs. 85
40. ONENESS OF DIVINITY	- Ratan Lal	Rs.100
41. PRASANTHI GUIDE	- R. Padmanaban	Rs. 50
42. SAI BABA AND NARA NARAYANA GUFA ASHRAM Part III	- Swami Maheswaranand	Rs. 20
43. SAI BABA GITA	- Al Drucker	Rs.240

44. SAI BABA'S SONG BIRD	- Lightstorm	Rs. 60
45. SAI BABA: THE ETERNAL COMPANION	- B. P. Misra	Rs.100
46. SATVIC FOOD & HEALTH (2nd Rev. Edition)	- Gerard T. Satvic	Rs. 40
47. SAI SANDESH	- Sai Usha	Rs. 50
48. SATHYA SAI'S AMRITA VARSHINI	- Sudha Aditya	Rs. 75
49. SATHYA SAI'S ANUGRAHA VARSHINI	- Sudha Aditya	Rs. 90
50. SATVIC STORIES	- Benjamin Kurzweil	Rs. 40
51. SAI HUMOUR	- Peggy Mason & Others	Rs. 70
52. SAI NAAMAAVALI	- Jagat Narain Tripathi	Rs. 90
53. SAI'S STORY	- Shaila Hattiangadi	Rs. 75
54. SELF REALISATION	- Al Drucker	Rs. 35
55. 70 QS & AS. ON PRACTICAL SPIRITUALITY AND SATHYA SAI BABA	- O.P.Vidyakar	Rs. 90
56. SPIRITUAL IMPRESSIONS A Bi-monthly Magazine		Rs.100
57. SPRINKLES OF GOLDEN DUST	- Jeannette Caruth	Rs. 65
58. SRI SATHYA SAI BABA AND WONDERS OF HIS LOVE	- John Elliott	Rs. 90
59. SRI SATHYA SAI CHALEESA	- B.P. Mishra	Rs. 15
60. SRI SATHYA SAI BABA PRAYER BOOK	- Sai Towers	Rs. 10
61. SRI SATHYA SAI BABA YOUNG ADULTS PROGRAMME	- L.A. Ramdath	Rs. 80
62. STUDY CIRCLES FOR DIVINITY	- Ross Woodward & Ron Farmer	Rs.390
63. TEN STEPS TO KESAVA	- Lightstorm	Rs.150
64. THE ARMOUR OF SRI SATHYA SAI	- O. P. Vidyakar	Rs. 10
65. THE DIVINE LEELAS OF BHAGAVAN SRI SATHYA SAI BABA	- Nagamani Purnaiya	Rs.100
66. THE GRACE OF SAI	- R. Lowenberg	Rs.120
67. THE HEART OF SAI	- R. Lowenberg	Rs.130
68. THE OMNIPRESENCE OF SAI	- R. Lowenberg	Rs.120
69. THE PHOENIX RETURNS	- Kristina Gale-Kumar	Rs.250
70. THE PROPHECY	- Barbara Gardner	Rs.120
71. THE SCRIPTURES ARE FULFILLED	- Kristina Gale-Kumar	Rs.160
72. THE THOUSAND SONGS OF LORD VISHNU	- Jeannette Caruth	Rs.150
73. THY WILL BE DONE	- C.D. Mirchandani	Rs. 90
74. WAITING FOR BABA (Reprint)	- V. Ramnath	Rs. 95
75. YOU ARE GOD	- M.N. Rao	Rs.150

FORTHCOMING PUBLICATIONS ...

01. A COMPENDIUM OF SAI BHAJANS	- R. Padmanaban
02. DIRECTORY OF MASTERS, SAINTS AND ASHRAMS IN INDIA	- R. Padmanaban
03. FOUNTAIN OF LOVE An Overview of Sathya Sai Water Supply Project	- R. Padmanaban
04. KRISHNAMURTHI AND THE FOURTH WAY	- Evan Gram
05. LOVE IS MY FORM VOL. I The Advent Pictorial Biography of Sri Sathya Sai Baba	- R. Padmanaban
06. PATH OF THE PILGRIM	- Richard Selby
07. SAI DARSHAN	- Vimla Sahni
08. STEPPING STONES TO OUR ETERNAL SAI SELF	- Lightstorm
09. WHO IS BABA?	- Margaret Tottle-Smith
10. UPBRINGING AND EDUCATION	- Gerard T. Satvic

Postal Charges

India: At the rate of 50 ps. per 100 gms plus Rs.12/- for Registration. Maximum 5 kg per parcel. Packing and Forwarding Charges per parcel Rs.40/-

Overseas: Sea Mail to North America, South America, Europe Rs.171/- for a 5 kg parcel, Singapore, Malaysia, New Zealand & Australia Rs.147/- plus packing and forwarding Rs.60/- per parcel

Air Mail Minimum postal Charges Rs.171/- per parcel to North and South America and Europe and Rs.147/- for Singapore, Malaysia, New Zealand and ustralia plus Rs.3/- for every 20 gms. Packing and forwarding charge Rs.60/- per parcel.

We accept your mail orders against bank drafts and credit cards.
Bank drafts should be drawn in favour of Sri Sathya Sai Towers Hotels P Ltd and payable in India.

✂— — —.— — — — — — — — — — — — — — — — —

To
Sri Sathya Sai Towers Hotels P Ltd.,
3/497 Main Road,
Prasanthi Nilayam 515 134, India

Dear Sir,
I herewith enclose the list of books required along with advance payment in full including postage and packing. Please despatch at your earliest

☐ Enclosed Bank draft for Rs..................

☐ Charge the total amount Rs................ ticked below to my Credit Card

☐ *Visa* ☐ *Mastercard* ☐ *DinersClub*

Card No ☐☐☐☐ ☐☐☐☐ ☐☐☐☐ ☐☐☐☐

Card Expiry Date.......................... Date of Birth M M DD Y Y ☐☐ ☐☐ ☐☐

Card Members Signature...

Name: Mr./Ms._____
Address_____
City_____Country_____
Phone: _____Fax: _____
E-mail:_____